I0493537

STOP KILLING

TIME

Get Shit Done, Crush Time Management and Achieve Crazy Productivity

DAVE CONION

Copyright © 2016 Dave Conion

All rights reserved. No part of this publication may be reproduced, distributed, or transmitted in any form or by any means, including photocopying, recording, or other electronic or mechanical methods, without the prior written permission of the publisher, except in the case of brief quotations embodied in reviews and certain other non-commercial uses permitted by copyright law.

www.conqueraverage.com

For queries, please email to

daveconion@conqueraverage.com

Fellow Warrior

A humble request to leave a review so we can improve on this journey to become our strongest version

Table of Content

About the Author

You must be thinking, who the fu*k is Dave Conion! Never heard of him before.

Okay, So I am Dave, I'm an entrepreneur, fitness model, martial arts professional and basically born to be awesome and why would I say something so cocky. That is because I believe so and that is what matters.

I think the biggest mistake we can ever make is to think small in a world that is full of infinite possibilities. But I have to say this wasn't the case ever since, I too had a tough time, depressed days, goalless years until the point I decided to question my existence in this world.

Since that day, I began a journey to leave the so-called Average life behind and unleash my true potential. I made a decision that I am not going to settle for anything but the best and help others along the way to discover their inner superhero that is waiting to be unleashed.

Introduction

Necessity to be a Super-Productivity Warrior

According to the Merriam-Webster Dictionary productivity is defined as, "The rate at which goods are produced or work is completed." In order for anyone to be truly successful in life, being super productive is absolutely essential.

Lack of productivity only results in reduced performance levels. Leading businessmen, thriving professionals and personally triumphant people have learnt the art of achieving things at a much shorter time frame than the rest of the world and it's exactly this trait that makes them a cut above the rest.

While working towards achieving their goals, people who are the genuinely productive kind end up giving their 100% focus to the job at hand. On the other hand, people who are less productive are constantly distracted and tend to shift focus very easily.

We live in a world that's filled with distractions and confusedness. Staying focused on the task at hand seems like an uphill task for most and they easily get carried away by the million distractions life has to offer.

The way technology is rapidly advancing, social media platforms, chatting software, our mobile phones and tablets, television sets and various other gadgets play the role of the biggest distractions in our lives.

We end up wasting hours on end glued to these gadgets and distractions and end up eating out of the time that we should spend focusing on important matters.

In order to be more productive and get less distracted, you need to start managing your time more efficiently. Time management plays a crucial role in increasing productivity. Keep in mind, being effective is very different from being busy.

So let's now understand what effective time management really is. Time management is nothing but how you plan, organise and prioritise your activities to give you maximum efficiency and productivity.

Now what most people don't realise is that productivity and time management go hand in hand, they are two sides of the same coin. As a wise man once said, "People use the hours of a day differently. But, the way you spend your time determines the quality of your life."

Are you looking to improve the quality of your mediocre, run of the mill life? Are you fed up of being just average? Well, then it's about time you started bringing about certain changes in your life.

Today we will discuss what you can do in order to maximise your productivity and achieve your full potential. How you can manage your time in a more efficient way so that you get maximum output.

Following these productivity tips will change your life in a positive and favourable way. You will put an end to the mediocrity personified life you're living and will get to indulge in the delectability of success.

We have compiled a list of productivity tips that will help you bring about these positive changes in your life. Some of these tips have been derived from the behavioural traits of the most successful businessmen and prosperous leaders across the globe and we are quite certain that they are going to help you too.

Chapter 1

The Productivity Warrior

I have a question for you. What is your definition of productivity?

That's what we're going to discuss today. How do you define productivity? But first of all why is it important?

You see productivity like success is one of those big topics that mean different things to different people. The Same way one person can define success is a lot of money, another person defines success with a lot of time. Productivity is exactly the same.

And there is, of course, an official definition, you can go to the dictionary and look it up, but that doesn't matter. What matters is your definition. And why it matters is, because there're tactics that you can use to get you to be more productive depending on your definition.

If you define it as A there are tactics that're going to help you get there. If you define it as B there are tactics that're going to help you get there as well. So I want to challenge you, take a couple of minutes and think, what does it mean for you to be productive?

How do you define productivity? There are generally 2 rules of thought and I'm going to show you both so you can see which one fits more with your definition. So let's get to it.

What are the 2 rules of thought when it comes to defining productivity?

Imagine that you have 4 hours, 4 hours for you to achieve 4 things and each one of them takes you 1 hour. And now you become more productive, maybe you increase your energy, you increase your motivation, and you become more focused. Whatever the case maybe.

What used to take you 4 hours, now takes you 3 hours, so you have 1 hour left. So what can you do with this one hour?

Option number 1 is, of course, you can take that one hour and you can do more work with it. Now you have one extra hour, now go out and achieve some more with that one extra hour. Sum-up these extra hours and you've got an extra day with a small productivity hack.

So increase your productivity, you increase your output, you do more work in the same amount of time as before.

Or

Option number 2: You can take that one hour and you can use it for something more enjoyable or something that's higher grade work. Maybe those 3 hours you spent on something you need to do, and now that 1 hour you're going to take and you're going to spend it on some high-quality work, writing or playing something or whatever the Fu*k it might be in your case.

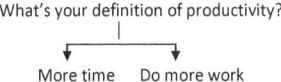

What's your definition of productivity?

More time   Do more work

So one is, you get to do more, the other one is you have more time left over. Maybe it is to enjoy and spend some time with your kids; maybe it's to go to the gym.

So I want you to take a couple of minutes, close your eyes and define what productivity to you is. Is it about getting more done so that you can get to your vision of success much faster, so you can get more done, so you can get to your goals faster?

Or is it so that you can have more time? More time for yourself, more time for your family, more time for what's enjoyable for you. And while you're at it, while you're defining what productivity means to you, I also want you to think about this other thing.

And I want you to answer this question. What does it mean to be productive? Where is the difference?

This one shows you what your definition of productivity is, but I also want you to think about what does it mean to be productive? And what you might discover, it's not so much about how much you get done but what you get done. Maybe you can get a million things done, but unless you go to the gym, unless you have some time, 30 minutes to go the gym you don't feel productive.

It doesn't matter how much you get done, as soon as you feel you don't get to the gym, nothing else matters. So if this is how you define productivity, whether it's the one thing or the five things you need to get done in order to feel productive, there are tactics that you can use to maybe schedule this thing in the morning. If going to the gym is what makes you feel productive, imagine if you put it in the morning and then you do your entire schedule. How would that feel?

Or maybe you define productivity as; you need to get a lot done. Maybe you've got to do a million things in order for you to feel productive, it's not about what you actually get done but about the quantity of everything you need to do. There're tactics that're going to get you there.

So I want you to think what does it mean to be productive? Is it a lot of things to get done or is it a few things that you absolutely have to get done. Once you define both of these your perspective is going to change.

Your mindset is going to be clear, you're going to know exactly what it is you need to do so you can figure out what tactics are going to get you there. And with how you define to begin productive, you can also use it as a benchmark. If productivity to you means that you have more free time instead of 9 hours of work and you now have 6, that's your benchmark.

You want to go from 9 to 6 and then maybe from 6 to 5 ½ you have some sort of a benchmark, or if you define productivity as you get more things done, I have a benchmark. You used to do 10 000 things, now you can 10001 things. So you are becoming more productive.

So once you figure out your definition of productivity, you can use it, A as a benchmark or B to figure out hey what is the tactics that're going to work for me. That's what matters, what works for you. Doesn't matter there're tactics out there that work for different people, what matters is if they work for you.

And in order to know that, you need to know your definition of productivity. I know this is a little bit of an out-there concept, but it really matters. Your mindset matters and in order for you to set your mindset you need to be absolutely clear on what productivity means to you. So take a couple of minutes, define productivity and define what it means to be productive.

Chapter 2

Magical Serum for productivity?

Ever wished that if you could find that one factor that is going to take your productivity through to the next level? Maybe something like a silver bullet?

Well if you ever wished to find one of those, today I am going to show you one that comes as close as possible to a silver bullet. Of course silver bullet, magical solutions to productivity do not exist but implementation intention is as close as it gets and today I am going to show you exactly how you can use it to boost your productivity and become successful by design.

What is this all about? It sounds way too complicated. Implementation intention, what is this? It is a very simple concept that is going to help you overcome a very simple but very destructive problem.

I will paint you a picture, has it ever been maybe it is a Tuesday afternoon and you know you need to exercise but you don't feel like it. Maybe you don't have enough energy, maybe you are not in the mood, and maybe you just don't feel like it.

That is when the problems become because so many things we don't feel like doing them. You know you have to do them and then you have to exercise your will power in order for you to do them.

If you don't have enough will power you just don't do it and then at the end of the day, you are like I should've exercised, I should've written that blog post, I should've done that video.

Then a) you don't do it so you don't actually achieve anything and b) you make yourself feel bad about it because you know you should've done it but you didn't do it.

All that is because things depend on your will power, if you don't have enough then you wouldn't be able to do the things that become hard to you. Implementation intention takes care of all that because it removes will power from the equation.

Implementation intention is a very fancy way of saying if something happens then I will do something else. If X happens then I will do Y. if it is 3 o clock I am going to exercise.

If I sit down on my desk I am going to write a blog post. If I set up the studio I am going to record a video. All this removes will power from the equation because now you know it depends on some sort of a cue.

If X happens then you need to do Y, removes the confusion, removes the when you have to do what. It removes the need to exercise your will power in order for you to take action.

Think of it like this, in all the buildings that you go, it says in the case of fire do these things. So if there is a fire, you need to do these things, you don't do them unless there is a fire and if there is a fire you do this.

It sounds a little bit complicated so let's break it down. There are 3 types of situations that you can use.

The first one is time-based.

The **First possibility** is to **attach a time to it**. So you know when the time comes you need to take a certain action.

A **second possibility** is that instead of time; **use a place** so when you sit down on a desk you do this. When you are in bed, you do this, when you go to this shop, you buy this. So instead of a time, you put in a place.

The **third possibility**, the third possible trigger is **an event**. So in case this happens then you are going to do Y. So let's say you put on your exercise clothes, and then it's a must for you to go to the gym. If you sit down then you need to take 10 deep breaths. If you get up then you need to stretch, whatever it might be in your case, whatever you are having a hard time with. If you attach one of these cues to whatever you are trying to achieve it becomes that much easier because there is no confusion.

There is no 'when do you need to do what', you just know if X is triggered then you do Y. this is how you start building a habit because the more you do it, one of these to achieve Y, it becomes a habit.

Then automatically when at 3 o clock you start going to the gym because you have done it so many times that now you have created a behaviour. You have created a habit and now you don't need to think as much, you don't need to work as hard in order to make Y happen.

Here is what I want you to do, here is how you can actually implement all this because all this is very nice but if you don't put it to use then nothing will change.

Pick one activity and I want you to pick a trigger for it whether it is a time, place, and event and here is what I want you to do next.

First, I want you to be very specific with your trigger and with your activity. Don't say I want to exercise in the afternoon, say if it is 3 o clock, the exact time I am going to go to the gym.

That is specific because it is going to help you make all this happen fast. A second thing that I need you to do is I want you to write it down. Take a piece of paper, a physical piece of paper not on the computer and write it down.

When 3 o'clock comes I am going to go to the gym. When I sit down at my computer I am going to write a blog post. When I come down I am going to wash my hands. When I finish brushing my teeth I am going to floss.

Whatever it is I want you to write it down. The third one, the one that makes all this possible is I want you to be realistic. This is all possible of you are honest with yourself, you got to be realistic.

If you haven't exercised for the last one year, thinking that this will take you to no exercise to exercising every single day is not realistic.

I want you to think like this, I want you to break it down in the smallest step possible. So instead of saying it is 3 o'clock I am going to exercise. I want you to think, if it is 3oclock I am going to put on my exercise clothes and I am going to go out, that's it.

This is combining the idea of implementation intention with the smallest amount of action you can take because let's face it if you are out there in your gym clothes. Let's say you are going to go for a jog or you are going to go to the gym.

So if you want to floss but you have never flossed before on a regular basis, start with the smallest possible realistic step. Once I am done brushing my teeth, so an event, I am going to floss one tooth.

Don't say I am going to floss all my teeth because if you haven't done it before, it is unrealistic to expect that it is just magically going to happen. Set the goal for I am going to floss one tooth that is it.

Or when I sit down on my desk, a place, I am going to write one sentence from the blog post. Chances are because you are being realistic because you are getting yourself over that hurdle of taking action the first time; you are not just going to write one sentence. You are not just going to floss one tooth; you are not just going to exercise for a minute.

You are going to do the full amount but if you say it is 3 o clock I am going to go exercise, you might be faced with too big of a hurdle and you might not take action whatsoever.

If you combine implementation intention with the idea of taking the smallest amount possible, the smallest amount of action as possible.

That is how you become successful by design. You do all these figures, you add figures, a time, a place, an event to everything you are having a hard time doing. You combine it with taking the smallest amount of action possible and you build your habits one by one.

You get more productive, you get more successful, and that is as close to a silver bullet as it comes. It is this simple but it works and that is what I am here to give you.

I am here to give you tactics; strategies that work so try it. Pick one activity that you are having a hard time with, attach some sort of cue to its whether it is a time, place, event, whatever fits the situation best.

Be specific, write it down and above all be realistic. If X happens I will do Y, do it for a week and I promise you that you will be hooked.

You will be so productive such that you will get done so many things that you will be absolutely hooked to this idea. Take action and start using it.

Implement this, implement it you are going to be hooked, have an amazing day.

Chapter 3

Grey Zone for Productivity

In this chapter, I am going to show how to get out of the grey zone and you might be thinking, what is the grey zone? The grey zone is where productivity goes to die.

The productivity in time management is a very black and white world; there are only 2 phases, the black and the white. What are they?

When it comes to productivity you are either working or you are relaxing, there is nothing else, there is no middle ground here. You are either at work and you are doing something productive or relaxing and you are gaining your focus, your energy, your motivation, your happiness, whatever it might be, so you can work some more.

The middle ground is what I call the grey zone; this is when you start daydreaming. You are working, and then all of a sudden you realize that you are not really working. Your focus is not there, your energy is gone and you are just daydreaming, you are thinking about something else.

Or you are relaxing but you are not really relaxing, you are not really enjoying yourself, you are thinking about work. Either of those are good, you either need to work or relax, it is a very black and white thing.

So before I show you how to get out of the grey zone, I want to show you what the reasons are for people who get in the grey zone. Once you understand the reasons you can understand how to fix them better.

Reason number one for being in the grey zone is good old fashion boredom. You do something and then you get bored or the thing was never fun and exciting and you just zone out.

Think about it, when you are fully engaged, when you are reading a book, when you are doing something that is super engaging, super fun, super cool whatever it might be, you zone out. You are fully present, you are there, you are watching the movie or you are writing that blog post or you are singing or you are performing whatever it might be, you are fully engaged, you are not bored, your focus is there.

As soon as you get bored for whatever the reason might be, you start to zone out, you start daydreaming, you start not being present, you start not being mindful.

Reason number one for being in the grey zone is good old fashion boredom. Reason number two is you eventually run out of energy. You work and then all of a sudden, you realize that your energy is gone.

Once your energy goes down, It brings down your creativity, your motivation, your focus everything follows your energy. So when you find yourself zoning out, daydreaming, being in the grey zone it's either because you get bored or you lack the energy.

So the question is, now you know the reasons, now you know what the grey zone is, how do you get out of it? I want you to show you a short term fix and a long term fix because you need to get out of the grey zone.

You either need to be working and when you are working; you need to be only working, fully engaged. Or you need to be relaxing and you are completely detached from work.

Once you fall in the middle, once you fall in between, you not really in one, you are not really in the other that is when your productivity is dead.

That is when you don't really relax; you don't really get anything done. Overtime this builds frustration because you will feel like you have worked all this time, you have spent 8 hours working but you didn't get done.

Or it was the weekend you felt like it was time to relax but on Monday, you don't feel so relaxed because you were thinking about work. The grey zone, so how do you get out of it?

The short term fix, if you catch yourself daydreaming the best thing to do is, of course, take a break. You are in the zone you are doing something then all of a sudden you realize you are not really in the zone, you are zoning out, take a break.

Take a 5-minute breather, you are better taking 5 minutes completely detaching yourself from work and then going back and getting the job done. Taking a break is going to allow you to detach yourself, it is going to bring your focus and you energy back up because you are taking the time to relax.

So the most important step here is to catch yourself daydreaming. Catch yourself, as you are working, always check with yourself, am I really working or am I just wasting time? Am I fully engaged with that thing that I am doing or am I thinking about something else?

If you catch yourself daydreaming, don't try to be a hero and be like no I am going to get back to it. Take a break, take a full 5-minute break, walk around, stretch your shoulders, and detach yourself from work.

Allow your focus to go back up, allow your energy to go back up and then resume work. If you cannot resume work, take a longer break.

You are better off sitting on the couch for 30 minutes at home or taking a 30-minute walk if you at work and completely detaching yourself than trying to force yourself to focus on something or force your energy to go when you don't have any energy to push yourself.

Short term fix, take a break but of course the short term fix is short, so how do you fix it in the long run? The long-term fix for getting out of the grey zone is adjusted by your work periods, what do I mean by that?

If you work for 50 minutes and then you are used to working for 50 minutes and then you catch that the last 10 minutes in your 15 minutes period, you zone out. You are not really working then maybe you need to lower your work periods to 40 minutes.

Or maybe you are doing 40 minutes and you need to lower them to 30 or maybe you don't even have a work period. Adjust you work periods, start slow, maybe put I am going to work for 20 minutes then I am going to take a break.

Once you get use to that, once you can work for a full 20 minutes, 20 minutes you work and nothing else, and then build up to 25, to 30, 35, and 45 whatever it might be in your case. Start slow and build your focus up because it might be that you are taking too long in between breaks.

Maybe you try to push yourself to work for an hour and a half without taking a break. So you run the risk of exhausting yourself and getting bored so maybe reduce it to 40 minutes, see how that works for you then slowly build that back up to an hour and a half.

Maybe you don't have a work period, make one start with 20 minutes, 30 minutes, 40 minutes but work in terms of time. Don't just go I am going to work until I get it done because that might take you more time, more energy, more motivation than what you currently have.

So you need to take a break, you need to restore your focus and your motivation and then you start work. So the long term fix for getting out of the grey zone is adjusted your periods, start small and build your way up.

That is the grey zone, the grey zone is in between work and relaxation when you are not working, you are not relaxing and you are not really getting stuff done. This is the worse type of time wasting because if you working but you are not really working, you exhaust yourself, you exhaust your focus but you don't really get anything done.

If you are relaxing but you are not really relaxing, you feel like you should have been relaxed because you took all this time, you took this break but mentally you are not recharged. So think about productivity as a black and white, there is no grey, there is no in between.

Either you work and you are fully engaged or you are relaxed and you are fully engaged with relaxation. As soon as you get in the middle, this is where your productivity goes down.

So boredom, lack of energy are the basic reasons of getting into the grey zone. The way to fix both of these is to take a break when you need one and adjust your work periods.

Maybe make them shorter or make them longer, you know what works best for you so you can eliminate this boredom and lack of energy. Once you get out of the grey zone, you either work or you relax that is when your productivity skyrockets. I want you to actually go through the steps, get out of the grey zone.

Chapter 4

You Only Have One Life

Take a moment to stop and evaluate yourself, your business, your time basically whatever you are currently doing with your life. Since we all only have one life to live, we need to make sure every moment counts.

Smart Idea Exercise 101:

Take a moment to draw a pie chart. Start by dividing up your time into percentages (out of 100%) according to these areas:

- Work
- Rest (sleep)
- Family
- Learning
- Fun and relaxation

Be honest with your evaluation. Then draw an open circle and put a point in the middle. From there, draw a line to the outer line. Now, as accurately as possible, divide up your chart according to your percentages listed above.

What does your chart look like? What slice of your pie is the largest? The answer to this question tells you how you have oriented your priorities.

Now, try this again with the categories from above. Write out what you would *like* your pie to look like (an "ideal" situation). This "ideal pie" is now your goal. You should, of course, determine if the allocations are realistic, but if they are, then consider what changes you need to make in order to move your "current pie" toward your "ideal" one. This could take years to achieve, but you now have a goal to aim for.

You Should Be Multiplying Your Time

Everyone loves a system that, once you get it to work, it does so seamlessly and without additional effort. Unfortunately, those types of systems don't tend to come about organically and generally take a lot of work to set up.

When you spend time focusing on implementing good time management skills, you can do so with an eye toward multiplying your time. A great example of this type of multiplication is scheduling out social media posts in advance. They are technically "working" for you throughout the week without you having to spend the time every day. Now, this does take an investment of time on the outset, but it reaps benefits long into the week (or month, depending on how far you schedule ahead).

You should always be looking for ways to multiply your time for the least amount of effort possible. It's not about being lazy but working smart.

Stress No More

Managing your time well means eliminating stress, or at least greatly reducing it. You will create a better quality of work; have more energy for what matters, and an all-around healthier outlook when you aren't working under stress. This, in and of itself, will create a better work environment, but it will also create a more productive environment. Working with little to no stress means you are able to enjoy your work. This can lead to greater innovation as well as a brighter outlook on your business.

Are You Efficient

Everyone is given the same twenty-four hours in a day. It's what we do with those hours that count. Efficiency is an important aspect of time management for your success.

To help get an accurate picture of your time, list out these things:

- What tasks do I need to complete?
  Think: daily, weekly, monthly, quarterly, yearly, bi-yearly

- How long should these tasks take?
  Give an estimation of how long these takes *should* take (not how long they actually do)

- What would I like to add on to this routine?
  Think: goals, dreams, new products/services

Now, looking at this list, write in how long these tasks *actually* take. You may need to do this over the course of a week while you evaluate your time spent. What you will notice as you map out your actual time versus your preconceived time is that there are a lot more interruptions on your time than you actually plan for. This is natural, but also probably throws off your time estimations.

The goal here is to gain an appropriate picture of what your time really looks like, not how you view your time looking on a "perfect" day. This helps with efficiency because, if you can see how your time is actually spent, you can schedule more accurately and plan in time for interruptions. You can also avoid feeling less productive by making your to-do list appropriate for your allotted time.

This type of efficiency helps you to look at what *is* instead of what *could* be. Being realistic about your time is the first step toward time management.

Time management is crucial to your business and work, no matter if you are the sole worker or the boss of several. You must be able to manage you own time well in accordance with others time, whether that's your employees or your customers. Take a look at the next chapter for a productivity warrior's tips and tricks for practical applications to hone your time management skills.

Chapter 5

Productivity Warrior Has his Tricks-
7 Productivity Tricks

After seeing the importance of managing your time well, we'll now take a look at some easily implemented tips and tricks to make the most of your time. These things, as with organizational ideas, aren't a cure-all. You still need to put in the hard work of evaluating what does and doesn't work as well as making appropriate adjustments to adapt these tips to your personal situation.

It's about You

The benefit of being an entrepreneur is that your business reflects you. That means your organization and time management needs to do the same. We understand that not everyone has the ability to craft their time in the way they would ultimately like.

However, to the extent that you can, it is important that you manage your time to what suits you and your customer's best. It may seem selfish but consider the fact that what make you successful is ultimately you. This revolves around the customer, but the idea (the "heart") comes from you. Take that into consideration.

Find Your Prime Time

As we've said, your business or work ethics is about you. You may not have the ability to move your working hours around, depending on your business, but you do have the luxury to work your free time around what best fits with your internal schedule.

Some people work well in the morning, others late at night, but no matter when your *prime time* is, you need to be working during that time!

Depending on your business hours, plan your schedule according to that and your prime time. Use that prime time to brainstorm business ideas, get creative about problem-solving, or work on organization.

Whatever the most pressing need for your business is, use your prime time toward that effort. In conjunction with the rest of these tips and tricks, you will have more energy and a better focus during that time.

Also, consider the best use of your prime time. If you have a morning commute, find a way to make that commute useful. You could be brainstorming ideas to a voice recorder, listening to an audio book for the entrepreneur, or completing phone calls through Bluetooth during this time.

Don't let parts of your workday slip by unused. It's important to use work time well, so that when you have free time you don't feel the need to still be working.

Smart Idea: Weather it's at six a.m. or eleven p.m., use your prime time to work on the innovative portions of your business. When you're at your best, you're inclined to be more creative and to produce your best work.

Before You Start

The most important time for you as an entrepreneur is to start your day (whenever this may be).

Use this time to sit down and plot out your to-do list. Remember our previous point about efficiency and be realistic with your time, but write it all out. It may be useful to have a white board on your desk or some other type of visual aid just so you know what you're doing and when.

At this point, depending on how your day typically plan out, it may be helpful to write in action items by time block.

If your job is more fluid, then just write out tasks, but we would encourage you to be intentional with prioritizing the items. Some things should be non-negotiable that need to be accomplished that day; others can be bumped to the next day, but don't make this a habit.

*Smart Idea: If you are constantly moving action items to the next day, you are overestimating your time in the day. Scale back what you need to accomplish. This is important because, at the end of the day, you don't want to feel as if you haven't accomplished things. This can lead to a type of depression and isn't actually an accurate picture of what you are accomplishing on a daily basis.

Use a Timer

There are times to ignore the clock and there are times to put it to good use. Make sure you know the difference!

After you've taken the time to plan out your day and prioritize, use a time to spur your creativity. Multi-tasking is great, but studies show that you don't accomplish as much when your focus is divided. Plan out your tasks for the day and set aside chunks of time toward each large task.

Once you've chosen a task, use a timer to alot time to that task, and *focus*. When the timer goes off, evaluate your progress. If you finish, great! If not, estimate how much more time you'll need and weight your options.

If you can reallocate time from another project, do so. If not, either leave that project to the end of your work day or move it to the top of your to-do list for the next day. This helps you learn and practice discipline with your tasks.

*__*Smart Idea:__ Start implementing the use of a timer with the strict idea that, whatever you don't fit into your allotted time frames must be moved to the next day. This helps to shape your boundary lines for your business. You'll start to find that a) you plan your time better and b) the world won't end if you don't get to that last project (usually).*

Take Away Distractions

In today's world, this idea is extremely difficult. There is always another email to be answered, call to take, texts to reply to, or Facebook messages coming in. It is easy to get distracted by the little things and realize they take up most of your time.

Establish a precedent now with regards to guarding your dedicated work time. Turn your phone to "do not disturb" (so your timer will still work but you won't be distracted), close out of your email, and don't open Facebook except for your scheduled times.

Working a solid hour without distraction will improve the quality of your work as well as the pace at which you can finish your work.

Overall, you will feel more accomplished after this. Though emails are important (especially with regards to customer service) you will find that they take up a lot of time. Be smart about scheduling in time to answer emails, return calls, and texts, and to check your social media.

Plan to Be Social

It may seem ridiculous to plan time to be on social media, but if it's not planned, then that's time taken away from another area of your priorities list.

When you plan in your time on Facebook, Twitter, Instagram, and Pinterest, you automatically go in with the idea that this is in association with work, not pleasure.

This is important for things like social media because they can become large time wasters. You will find yourself scrolling through endless feeds on Facebook, completely forgetting why you were on there in the first place.

The same can be said for blog reading for research. This is a good action and you can gain knowledge from it, but you must be cautious of how easy it is to waste time doing what appears to be helpful but is, in fact, a distraction. Use a timer while on social media and make sure it is part of your scheduled day.

Smart Idea: Consider breaking up these media times into ten or fifteen-minute increments throughout the day. This will keep you "current" without overtaking your day.

Rest Up

There needs to be a large emphasis on rest when considering your time management. This is important because no one is a machine.

Being human means there is a deep-seated need for rest and taking breaks. This is becoming increasingly more important as research shows that standing for portions of the day (if you work at a desk) can help improve your health as well as your productivity.

While planning out your day, include times for adequate breaks. This includes ten to fifteen-minute breaks as well as a lunch break. During these breaks make sure you stand up, stretch, and actually, rest.

Stepping away from a project can help improve your perspective and stamina when you come back to it. Just make sure you leave any project or work with clearly defined notes as to where you're heading next. There's nothing worse than walking away and not remembering your direction after the break.

Smart Idea: *Combine a few of these tips! Take your social media and rest breaks while standing near or at your desk. Don't do this for every break, but occasionally.*

Own Up to It

The last thing to consider when focusing on time management is to understand the reality that sometimes you cannot accomplish everything you want to. You may have had the best of intentions when setting out to create you priority list for the day or week, but planning for the unplanned is hard enough without being able to keep up with your normal day-to-day business requirements.

Allow yourself a bit of slack when it comes to accomplishing your goals. As we've already stated, if you find you are constantly overestimating the amount of work you will finish or underestimating the amount of time it will take to complete a task, revaluate. This is not admitting defeat; it's a smart business move.

This may also mean adjusting your overall goals. If you've set certain goals for the next six months but are realizing they may not be possible, adjust for that. What is most important is that you do the best you can with the things you already have in place before adding anything to your schedule or your business.

Time management and productivity take time to plan out, but in the end, you will reap the benefits for having set aside that time. Be through and use helpful tools like timers, spreadsheets, and online time-trackers to ensure you are making the best use of your time. At the end of the day, don't mourn the incomplete tasks, but give yourself credit for what you *did* accomplish. Use those unfinished tasks to fuel your next day's to-do list.

Lastly, you will likely find that, when you track your time, your unproductive hours are spent on things that don't add to your relaxation or overall well-being. Use your free time to spend with your family and friends, working out and eating healthy, and spending time actually resting. You will feel more rejuvenated for having spent an actual day of than spending half an hour here and there taking a break.

Chapter 6

7 Productivity Tips you should consider

Managing those Damn Emails

We live in a world where technology is constantly advancing at the speed of a jet plane. Our email accounts are pretty much synchronised with every gadget we own, making our emails accessible everywhere and all the time. This pretty much results in non-stop beeping and buzzing of our phones and gadgets every time a new email is received, which further results in the temptation to check the mail. If you're going to keep checking your phone or tablet is going to keep buzzing with new emails every hour, it is going to prove to be a great distraction for you. Each time you unlock your phone to read a new email, you're going to end up wasting a certain amount of time reading it and responding back. This, in turn, will directly affect your productivity. So allot a certain time of the day to read and respond to your emails. Turn off the email alerts on your gadgets to avoid getting tempted to check the mails. This will help you in keeping your productivity levels steady.

Dump the Idiot Box

Most people watch an average of 3 hours of television a day. That adds up to almost 21 hours a week. If you reinvest that time in work and things of importance, it will boost up your productivity to a great extent. Get rid of the television set in your office, study room and any place where you work. Gradually cut down the number of hours you spend in front of your television and start using that time wisely.

Clear the Clutter

In order to be super productive, you need to be in an atmosphere that's completely clutter free. If your work place has stacks of papers, files, books and other documents lying around in every nook and corner, it's really going to mess with your productivity. What most people don't realise is that clearing out clutter has numerous psychological and other benefits. For one, clearing clutter has proven to reduce and prevent anxiety in people. Reduced anxiety further results in greater productivity. Secondly, a mess free atmosphere plays a vital role in increasing concentration and focus. Increased levels of focus and concentration increase productivity levels too, which further result in greater performance and results. Lastly, clearing clutter also proves to be a great way to boost one's self-esteem, which further results in increased levels of productivity too. Clutter proves to be a constant reminder of tasks and jobs that are pending and incomplete. You don't constantly need these reminders as they tamper with your self-esteem and overall productivity. Thus, ensure that you get rid of anything and everything that's unnecessary from your desk or workplace to increase your levels of productivity.

Exercise Daily

You're probably wondering, "How can exercising have any kind of impact on my productivity?" Well, not only do the two correlate, but exercise has also proven to be one of the world's greatest tools for productivity. Exercising increases the energy levels in your body. Increased levels of energy are directly proportional to your productivity levels. If you're exhausted and tired, your productivity levels are also going to be extremely low. On the other hand, if you're refreshed, rejuvenated and highly energetic after a good workout, you're going to be super productive. However, do keep in mind that just being energetic isn't enough, channeling that energy in the right direction is also very important to increase your productivity levels.

Motivation is the key

Often our productivity levels take a big plunge due to lack of motivation. Motivation is absolutely essential to increase your productivity. You can keep yourself motivated by reading motivational articles or books, listening to audiobooks or podcasts, setting goals for yourself and ensuring that you work towards the completion of them and being around people who motivate and inspire you. So do whatever it takes to keep yourself motivated, wake up every morning with a strong and overpowering sense of determination that boosts your confidence and in turn your productivity levels and allows you to sleep at night with an overwhelming feeling of satisfaction for having to be super productive.

Maintain a To-Do List

Successful and productive people across the globe have one thing in common, they maintain and follow a daily to-do list. If you truly want to increase your productivity levels and enhance your performance, maintaining a to-do list is essential. Without a to-do list, your mind will become scattered and the possibility of you forgetting the important tasks you need to complete are very high. A to-do list will help you go through your tasks and your day in a systematic and organised manner, thereby resulting in maximum productivity and better levels of performance. So get yourself a notebook and start jotting down the tasks you need to complete on a daily basis.

Say No like a Boss

Your need for approval aside, it's about time you stopped being a people pleaser and learn how to say no to the things that are of no benefit to your overall growth and well-being. If you keep saying yes to everything and everyone and end up indulging in the things that don't interest you, you will never have enough time to get the things you really want to be done. In order to be super productive, you need to stop being a pushover and focus only on those things that are of top priority and great importance to you.

Chapter 7

Warrior Way Goal Planning

We've looked at the importance of organization and time management for the entrepreneur, but within these two areas we touched a little on establishing goals and thinking through the extent of your organization. We'll spend just a little additional time here on these two things as they relate to the organization and optimizing your time management.

Goals worth Achieving

After a business plan has been created, business goals are next in line of importance to the forward motion of your business. Without clearly defined goals coming out of identified strengths and weaknesses of your business as it is now, you won't be moving forward. This can be intimidating, establishing the future of your business, but it is crucial for forward movement. Don't worry, though; long-term goals, though firm, don't have to be a completely set in the stone idea. They can, however, create a healthy motion for your business.

We recommend you set aside at least half a day if not longer to goal-plan for your future. This should come after you've established your business plan. You'll want to have paper or a white board handy to map out the trajectory of your business.

Walk through these steps:

1. **Start with your business plan and tagline.**
   Take a few minutes to remind yourself of why you started your business in the first place, the "heart". This is the essence of you business and should fuel everything you do. If it isn't true to where your business is today, adjust it to fit the new perspective. It is important to keep this up-to-date.
   In some cases this could mean rebranding. In others, just a re-focusing of priorities.

2. **Brainstorm/Think ahead.**
   It's time to do a little dreaming. This is a great opportunity to let your imagination run

wild. Don't restrict yourself to what you *think* is possible but what you would like to be possible. This is a crucial step because it takes away the societal and realized boundaries and instead lets you see what you actually hope for.

3. **Narrow your focus.**
   Take the things you brainstormed, organize them, and start to weed out things that either isn't likely to happen or are not possible within the next five years. These aren't completely taken out of the realm of possibility, but they aren't factors at this point either (possibly due to money, time, or other constraints).

4. **Map it out.**
   Now, take the things from your narrowed focus and begin to organize them into realistic categories depending on how far out you think they will need to be planned. If you currently run a small store and wish to have a chain of five up and running in the future, you wouldn't put that goal a year away. That's upwards of a five to ten-year goal. Just make sure you are realistic about these plans.

5. **Get specific.**
   This is very important when it comes to goal creation. If you aren't specific to the goal, its needs in order to be reached, and a plan as to how you will get there, you aren't likely to reach that goal. Work from the outward in (years wise) and become more and more detailed the closer you get to where you are at right now. The closer out each goal is, the more steps you should create. Don't make these steps so impossible that you are never achieving them. Some will naturally be harder, but be sure to be realistic too.

6. **Work your goals.**
   This is the part where you get to implement your goals and the steps to achieving them. This may require a directional change of your business, daily routine changes, or even reallocation of time and/or money to achieve these goals. Do these things with your goals clearly in mind.

Make sure to schedule regular check-ups to see how you are doing with relation to your goals. Are your timelines realistic? Are you feeling overwhelmed by what you have chosen to accomplish? Are your goals too easy? Make the time to evaluate and adjust as necessary.

Smart Planning

We can talk a lot about planning, but if it's not smart planning, it will only be a waste of time. What we mean by smart planning is that it is concise, cost effective, takes into account your tagline or business focus, and doesn't take over your time.

When you goal plan, you can get wrapped up in the future of you business and forsake the current state of it. That will only bring trouble in the present and the future.

When you plan ahead for your business, make sure your plans are leading you toward a goal and aren't so difficult to implement that you or your customers become frustrated.

The difficulty in planning and organizing is that it will affect your customers during the adjustment time to a new system. If changes are made that affect your customers, be sure to inform them along the way of new policies, procedures, prices, and practices.

Be careful to care for them during this time so that they aren't feeling left behind with regards to any new direction or idea.

It's important to note here that any changes put into place should consider your customer. The marketing aspect of your business should afford you a good look into what your clientele likes and wants. Any change you make should be in line with that.

Better Organization

For every organizational procedure put in place, there are positives and negatives. The discussion of the best future organization centres on the fact that you won't know if your organizational systems are working until you put them in place and allow them to do just that, work. We've talked a lot about revaluating, but that's not just a buzzword. You have to allow time for a system to fall into working order before seeing its results.

Now, obviously you won't want to let a failed system go on failing just to meet a stated time-goal, but you should make sure to give adequate time to see the ups and downs. There will likely need to be small adjustments made, but let your system fall into place before deciding if it works or not.

Once you've given it adequate time (anywhere from three to six months) revaluate. Are the systems you put in place working? What's meeting your needs? What isn't? What's wrong? What's working well?

Ask these questions then consider future systems you may want to put into place. Maybe that's additional shelving, relabeling everything, or a total remodel of your space. These things may not be crucial, but they are good to consider in addition to new ways to keep your spaces organized. Leave room for growth while still making sure that what you have in place is doing a good job.

Being an entrepreneur, you are constantly faced with the reality of the here and now. There are challenges you must overcome without having to consider your organizational skills or time management, but neglecting their importance is a big mistake. Just a little time spent organizing your space and time will greatly increase your productivity while decreasing your stress. This will not only affect you and your personal stress level but also the relationships you will have with your clients.

Realize that you absolutely *can* live a fulfilling and relaxed life as an entrepreneur by taking the proper precautions on your time. Step into better organization and time management today, and realize a brighter future for your business tomorrow.

Conclusion

The Productive Warrior Unleashed

As Paul J. Meyer once said, "Productivity is never an accident. It is always the result of a commitment to excellence, intelligent planning, and focused effort."

If you truly wish to become successful, achieve your goals and fulfil all your dreams, you need to completely shift your focus on maximising your productivity and increasing your performance levels.

You need to make a commitment towards managing your time better and putting in sincere efforts towards achieving your goals. You need to start making things happen instead of just waiting for them to happen.

There isn't a man in history who has acquired success and fame without being productive. So stop being lazy and quit praying for a miracle. The only person who can make things happen in your life is you.

There's no short cut to success and the only way to reach the top is by being productive and working hard. Be dedicated to working hard, be committed to achieving your goals, set aside distractions and keep yourself motivated, these qualities will help you become the person you want to be.

Most importantly, when you find yourself slipping, always remind yourself that "A bird sitting on a tree is never afraid of the branch breaking because her trust is not on the branch but on her own wings. Always believe in yourself."

Self-Assessment

1) I am very clear about what I want out of life

❏ Hell Yeah! ❏ Maybe ❏ Uhh! No

2) I know exactly the amount of money I want to earn

❏ Hell Yeah! ❏ Maybe ❏ Uhh! No

3) I am obsessed with success.

❏ Hell Yeah! ❏ Maybe ❏ Uhh! No

4) I believe that I will turn my financial goal into reality.

❏ Hell Yeah! ❏ Maybe ❏ Uhh! No

5) I spare time every day to train my mind for success.

❏ Hell Yeah! ❏ Maybe ❏ Uhh! No

6) I believe in providing value in the lives of people.

❏ Hell Yeah! ❏ Maybe ❏ Uhh! No

7) I take consistent action towards my goal.

❏ Hell Yeah! ❏ Maybe ❏ Uhh! No

8) I have written goals to keep me on track.

❏ Hell Yeah! ❏ Maybe ❏ Uhh! No

9) I believe I deserve all the success in life.

❏ Hell Yeah! ❏ Maybe ❏ Uhh! No

10) I have work ethics of a millionaire.

❏ Hell Yeah! ❏ Maybe ❏ Uhh! No

Scoring

Hell Yaa! You get 1 point._____

Maybe, you get 2 points._____

Uhh! No, you get 3 points._____

This is your Final Score. _____

Scored between 10 to 15 points: Congrats, We have a good news, you are in the right direction towards achieving your personal success. The below techniques will strengthen your beliefs and boost in achieving your goals. Keep fighting and you will be victorious.

Scored between 11 to 24: You are on the right track in some important aspect but lacking in some. Find your weakness and take consistent actions on working towards improvement in those areas.

Scored between 25 to 30: You have either not begun your journey towards personal success or working in the wrong direction. You need to analysis yourself, your goals and work towards them as if your life depends on it. Start working on your principle straight away and you are bound to achieve the success you desire.

Finding your Purpose

I am going to make you a money making machine!! The only thing that separates the rich from the poor is their mindset. Answer the below question. When you have completed these questions you will have a clear idea of what you desire. You are only limited by the limitation of your own mind. Dream big

What is the exact amount of money you want to make?

_____

_____

What value would you provide in return? (Remember you have to provide in order to receive)

_____

_____

Set a specific timeline, when do you want the money you desire?

_____

_____

What is that one thing you are passionate about?

_____

_____

Find your options are available in order to achieve your goals?

_____

_____

Design an action plan of how you intend on achieving your goals? Write down what step you will take this very moment to work towards your goal keeping our timeline in mind. (You won't do it tomorrow, stop being lazy and do it right now!)

_____

_____

_____

_____

Combine all the answer from above question and again write them down below. (Writing them down again will validate them and make your desire stronger)

_____

_____

_____

_____

Review these goals every f**king day. This is not given to you by your boss, your parents, or your friends. This is what you want out of your life and you have to do whatever it takes to achieve it.

Finding your Reasons

Every one of us encounter situations wherein we become unfocused, doubtful, deviate from our goals and may eventually end up quitting. Writing done 5 reason will bind you to achieve the goals you desire.
It could be to quit your boring job, travel the world, build a business, or buy a fucking Lamborghini! This will provide you the motivation and vision to keep your ass moving.

Write down 5 reasons why it is a must for you to achieve your goals.

1) _____

2) _____

3) _____

4) _____

5) _____

Before You Go

"If you enjoyed my book, it would be greatly appreciated if you left a review so others can receive the same benefits you have. Your review will help me see what is and isn't working so I can better serve you and all my other readers even more on this journey to become our strongest versions"

Do check out other books as well

Dave Conion Author central

Thanks again for taking the time to download and read this book. I really do appreciate it!

Best Wishes,

Dave Conion

www.ingramcontent.com/pod-product-compliance
Lightning Source LLC
Chambersburg PA
CBHW071829200526
45169CB00018B/1297